Bing Bang Boing

Bing Bang Boing

Poems and drawings by
Douglas Florian

Harcourt Brace & Company
San Diego New York London

Library of Congress Cataloging-in-Publication Data
Florian, Douglas.
Bing bang boing: poems and drawings/by Douglas Florian.—1st ed.
p.   cm.
Summary: An illustrated collection of more than 170 nonsense verses.
ISBN 0-15-233770-9
1. Children's poetry, American. [1. American poetry.]
I. Title.
PS3556.L589B56   1994
811'.54—dc20   94-3894

Printed in Singapore

First edition

A B C D E

The illustrations in this book were done in
pen and ink on Strathmore drawing paper.
The display type was set in Belwe Medium and
the text type was set in Weiss by
Thompson Type, San Diego, California.
Scanning by Bright Arts, Ltd., Singapore
Printed and bound by Tien Wah Press, Singapore
Production supervision by Warren Wallerstein and David Hough
Designed by Kaelin Chappell

For Allyn Johnston

First

First things first.
Last things last.
Hours
    pass
        slowly.
Years pass fast.

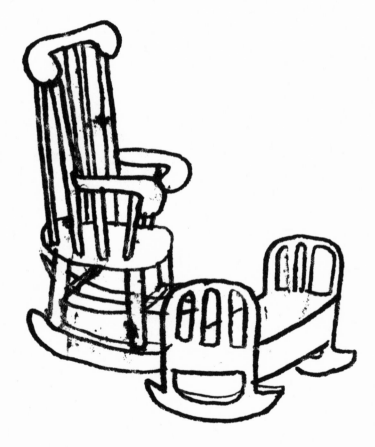

Pages

The pages in a book
Sit glued and bound.
I turn the pages,
And they turn me around.

Book Crooks

They stole my pants,
Th y st le her purse.
T ey stol some let ers
From th s verse.

Mr. Cook

Mr. Cook's in love with books —
He piles them wall to wall.
On breezy days they gently sway,
And with a sneeze they fall.
He reads all day, great novels and plays,
Reciting to Mrs. Cook.
But as he feared, she's disappeared.
And who knows where to look?

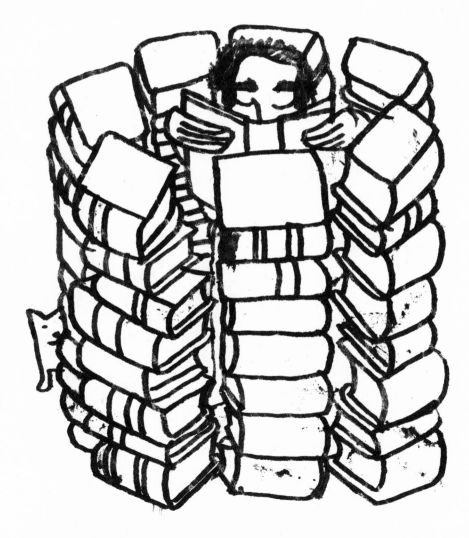

Strange Change

An enterprising wizard
Turned Aunt Fay into a lizard.
She looks just like a dinosaur —
Much better than she did before.

What a Mad Magician Did to Me

He cut me in half —
Just for a laugh.
He cut me in thirds —
The pain's beyond words.
He cut me in eighths —
I'm in dire straits.
He cut me in twelfths —
I'm not my old self.
He cut me in thirtieths —
Oh, boy, did it hurtieth.
He cut me to bits —
I'm out of my wits.
He cut me to shreds —

I'm dead.

If Your Car Goes

If your car goes *clippety-clump*
Each time it hits a bippety-bump,
And on a turn you hear a *clunk* —
A clinking, clanking, clunking *plunk* —
Maybe . . .
A turtle's hiding in your trunk.

Grandpa Owns a Rocking Chair

Grandpa owns a rocking chair —
He keeps it by the cellar stair.
For Grandpapa would rather hike
Cross-country on his motorbike.

My Robot

I have a robot
Do the dishes,
Phone my friends,
Bone the fishes.
Rub my back,
Scrub the floors;
Mop the kitchen,
Open doors.
Do my homework,
Make my bed;
Catch my colds,
Scratch my head.
Walk the dog,
Feed the cats;
Hit my sister,
Knit me hats.

Do my laundry,
Clean my room;
(Boy, he's handy
With a broom).
Comb my hair,
Darn my socks;
Find my lost toys,
Wind my clocks.
Mix me milk shakes,
Fix my bike;
Buy me all
The things I like.
Grill me hot dogs,
Guard my home —
Who do *you* think
Wrote this poem?

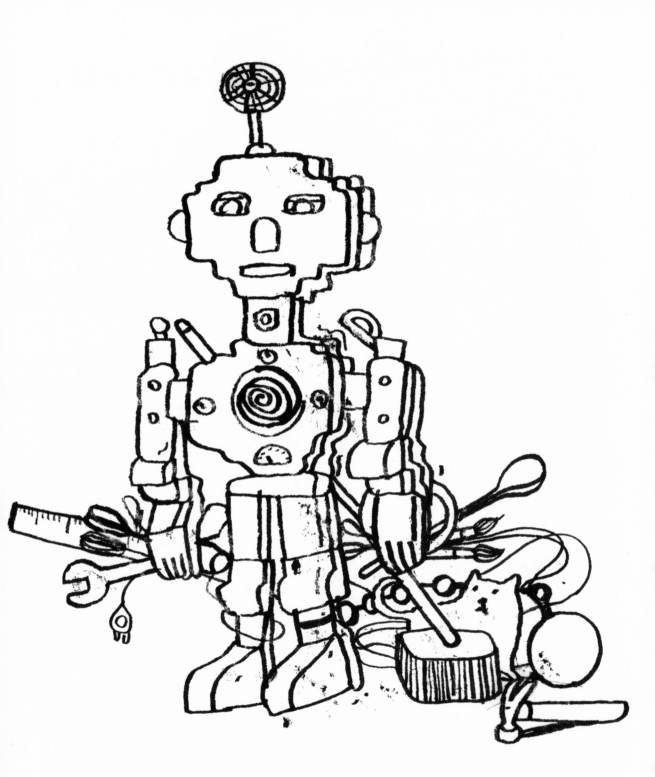

Male Mail

Willard wishes to travel far —
Mailed himself to Zanzibar.
Parcel postage was his end.
Forgot to stamp: PLEASE DO NOT BEND.

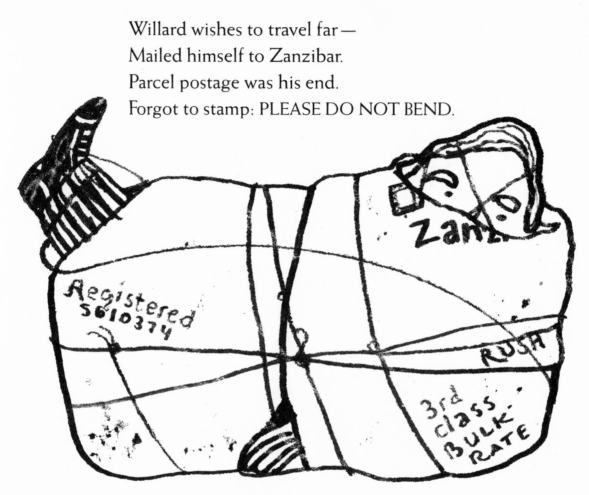

Cake Mistake

Mother made a birthday cake,
For icing she used glue.
The children sit so quiet now,
Andchewandchewandchew.

Walking School

They sent me off to walking school
So I could learn the proper rules.
Like how to keep my shoulders straight
And stepping with a rhythmic gait.
Point both my feet out ten degrees —
Don't sway my back or bend my knees.
Till now I find I'm walking great —

Except my head's two seconds late.

Monday the Baby Learned How to Walk

Monday the baby learned how to walk.
Tuesday the baby learned how to talk.
Wednesday she learned to write her name,
To knit a sweater and build a frame.
Thursday she learned to read a book,
To use a computer, to shop and cook.
Friday she learned to plug a leak,
To translate Russian into Greek.
Saturday she learned to fix a tire,
To drive a bus, to sing in choir,
To stage a play, to play the lyre.
Sunday the baby plans to retire.

Self Serve

Last night I dreamed I saw myself
Sitting on the market shelf,
On sale for seven fifty-three.
I'm glad they thought
That much of me.

Prim and Proper Mrs. Preet

Prim and proper Mrs. Preet
Lived a life so very neat.
Even as a little child,
She had all her scribbles filed.
Filed names and filed places,
Filed addresses and new faces.
Filed friends and filed foes,
Filed ways to blow her nose.
Then when Mrs. Preet grew older,
Filed herself inside a folder —
Completely, neatly classified.
And there she stayed until she died.

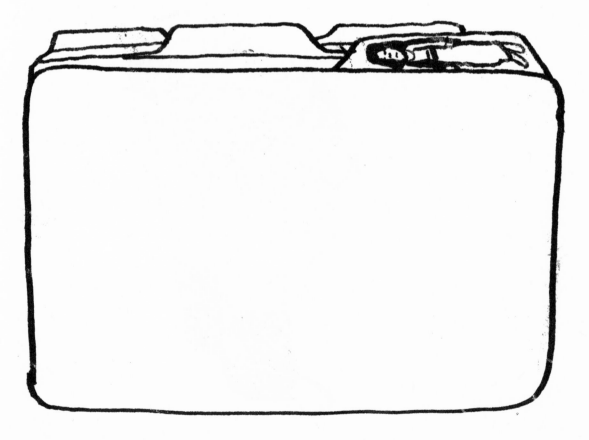

Twins
Twins

Fred and Ted are twins.
Fred and Ted are twins.

They always dress the same.
They always dress the same.

Teddy tears the curtains.
Teddy tears the curtains.

Freddy gets the blame.
Freddy gets the blame.

Heady

It's said two heads are better than one,
And three heads are better than two.
　　But having three heads
　　Is something I dread,
Just between me and you.

Genny Glubber

Genny Glubber's fat like blubber.
She has knock-knees made of rubber.
Birds nest in her stringy hair.
Her nose is long; her head is square.
Her eyes are crossed; her teeth are loose.
Her neck is longer than a goose.
She has two ears as big as plates.
She wears green shoes (size fifty-eight).
Her legs are scrawny, like a chicken.
Her face leaves people panic-stricken.
All day long I'm thinking of her —
Genny Glubber, how I love her.

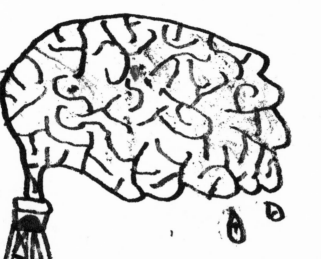

Drilly

Drill for oil,
Drill for gas,
Drill for purple Plexiglas.
Drill for copper,
Drill for lead.
Drill for brains inside your head!

Double Trouble

I trucked my troubles out of town
To some address unknown.
But come and look!
My troubles took
The trouble to come home.

Hailstones

Hailstones big as marbles,
Hailstones two feet wide.
Hailstones big as boulders —
Better stay inside.

Swallowed Pride

They said that I'd better
Swallow my pride.
So inside a large saucepan,
My poor pride I fried.
I cut it to pieces
And started to feed. . . .
Tomorrow I'm planning
To gobble my greed.

An Apple a Day

An apple a day
Keeps the doctor away.
But if you eat eleven,
You'll soon go to heaven.

Send My Spinach

Send my spinach
Off to Spain.
Parcel post it
On a train.
Mail it,
Sail it
On a ship.
Just don't let it
Touch my lip.

Food Mood

I'm out of broccoli,
Very luckily.
A carrot stick
Makes me sick.
I'm too fickle
To eat a pickle.
A dish with radish
Gets me madish.
I always balk
At a celery stalk.
Brussels sprouts
Are best thrown out.
And I like spinach
When it's finished.

27

Shoddy Body Shop

I took my car to a body shop
To patch a scratch on a fender top,
To change the oil and check the brakes,
But they worked on me by some mistake.
They oiled my joints and greased my hair,
Then filled my left foot full of air.
They wiped my glasses and washed my trunk,
And cleaned my crankcase of all gunk.
They patched my scratches up with putty
(The same exact shade as my body).
In steely blue they sprayed my back,
Till I shone like a Cadillac.
They snapped two wipers on my eyes
And gave my skin a Simonize.
They screwed a mirror on my side,
Then bolted bumpers to my hide.
They glued two taillights to my heels
And gave me four steel-alloy wheels.
They put new brake pads on my feet,
Then rolled me out onto the street,
Placed a price tag on my head,
And sold me to a guy named Fred.
So now in Fred's garage I wait —
For me the time is far too late.
But you must listen! You must stop!
Don't take your car to a body shop!

Drive On

Let's drive in the car
Till we run out of road,
Till we run out of gas,
Or the tires explode.
Let's drive all the morning
And all afternoon,
And never turn back
Till we get to the moon.

The Spotted Spee

If you should see
The Spotted Spee,
You'd better run and hide.
For though the Spee
Is two feet tall,
It's fifteen miles wide.

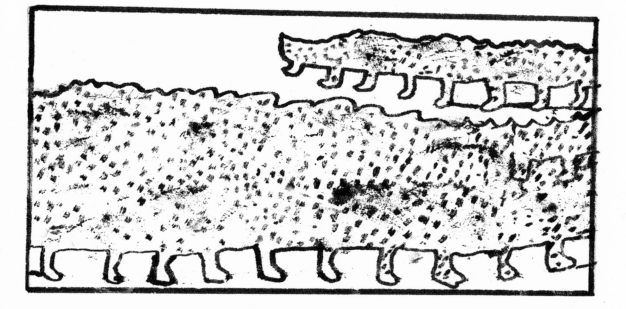

My Rocket-Powered Roller Skates

My rocket-powered roller skates
Go very fast and *very* straight.
They're dual-cam and turbo-prop —
If I could just get them to stop!

Gideon Giles

Gideon Giles has seven smiles —
He grins from cheek to cheek.
But when he wants to brush his teeth,
It takes him half a week.

Ping-Pong Poem

The
In-
This
Pong
Bounce
And
Like a

words
side
Ping-
poem
back
forth
metronome.

Uncle Reggs

Uncle Reggs is fond of eggs —
He juggles them between his legs.
He rolls them down the street with wheels
And hangs them high in steel mobiles.
He uses them to stop a door
Or drops them from the seventh floor.
He paints them all assorted hues,
Then slips them into people's shoes.
He wraps them up in yellow ribbons
And feeds them to giraffes and gibbons.
He broils, boils, bakes, and beats them,
But never
Ever
Ever
Eats them.

Aunt Esther

A beast bit my aunt Esther
And managed to ingester
But couldn't quite digester
'Cause her dress was polyester.
Now crazy old Aunt Esther
Is my favorite ancestor.

I'm in the Mood for Mud

I'm in the mood for mud —
I'm mad for sloggy, boggy crud.
I wish to wallow in a mire,
To slip and slosh my heart's desire.
To slide and slop inside the slush,
To run amok amid the mush.
And when I'm done I'll run upstairs,
Where in the tub I'll wash my hairs,
And back and legs and arms and chin,
Then run back in the mud again.

Sloppy Girl

Suzie is a sloppy girl —
Her clothes are on the floor.
She'd like to go to school today
But just can't find the door.

Trouble Bubble Gum

What DO you do with bubble gum
When it's no longer sweet?
Do you stick it 'neath the table?
Would you throw it in the street?
Can you weave it in a basket?
Will you save it in a jar?
Or else use it as a gasket
In your uncle Isaac's car?
Should you patch it on flat tires?
Or else plug a leaking pipe?
Could you hold together pages
Of a book report you type?
You may hang it from the ceiling.
You may mail it overseas.
Just make sure your ancient bubble gum
Is very far from me.

If I Eat More Candy

If I eat more candy . . .
My teeth will fall out.
My gums will turn green
Like the rest of my mouth.
The dentist will drill me,
While I scream in pain,
A dozen long holes
That spill into my brain.
The stench of my breath
Will kill birds in the air —
But
This candy's so good
That I really don't care!

City Rush

See the city rush,
Feel the city crush.
Busy people in a hurry —
See them scatter,
Watch them scurry.
All day long they flit and flee
To places they don't want to be.

Sister Story

Three miserly sisters named Brown
Went shopping all over the town.
    They went in a store
    For an hour or more
And came out in a single new gown.

An Eye

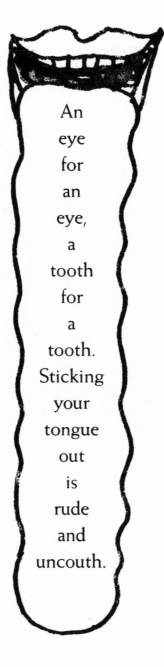

An
eye
for
an
eye,
a
tooth
for
a
tooth.
Sticking
your
tongue
out
is
rude
and
uncouth.

Ink Sink

I climbed into the kitchen sink
To take a bath in orange ink,
And though my skin was squeaky clean,
I looked just like a tangerine.

I tucked my knees, I held my feet,
And slowly tumbled down the street.
For fourteen blocks I whirled and rolled,
Then landed near a salad bowl,

Where I was peeled and smartly sliced,
Then into little cubes was diced.
Into the air I turned and tossed,
Then swam beneath vinaigrette sauce.

So now in pieces here I think
About my bath in orange ink.
It was a foolish thing to do.
Next time I'll bathe in turquoise blue.

Pencilly

The pencil is a splendid thing
For which there's no replacer.
But better than the pencil is
The little pink eraser.

Monster Home

A monster made its very home
Inside the middle of this poem.
This monster loved to gobble words —

Of this poor poem it ate two-thirds.

What I Want for My Birthday

A teddy bear
An antelope,
A ninety-four-inch telescope.
A clarinet
A kettledrum,
Ten thousand sticks of bubble gum.
A tennis court
A two-by-four,
A bony-plated dinosaur.
An iron bridge
A bust in granite,
A recently discovered planet.
A symphony
A subway car,
A sixty-five-pound candy bar.
A matzo ball
A bodyguard —
AND DON'T FORGET TO SEND THE CARD!

Achoo!

A mouse was chewing
Muenster cheese,
When suddenly
It chanced to sneeze.
A little sneeze,
A little mouse —
It blew the roof
Right off the house.

Izzy Eats Ice Cubes

Izzy eats ice cubes —
A very nice way
To guarantee getting
Three square meals a day.

No Nose

Has
anyone
seen my
nose? It
must be lost,
I suppose. It
isn't on my face
or head — I guess
I lost it in my bed
whilst I was dreaming
late last night. Now I
must look an awful fright,
and though I look with all
my might, my nose has disappeared from sight. Not in
the bed sheets or my clothes —
Just where do missing noses
goes? Has anyone seen
my nose?

My Nose Knows

I hate it when I blow my nose
And tortoises fall on my toes.
And if I blow my nose again,
I know I'll see a railroad train.
I fear that if I puff once more,
I'll clearly huff a dinosaur.
And when this whiff I do repeat,
I'll blow out Forty-second Street.
I'll blow no more,
I fear the worst —
Perhaps I'll blow
The universe.

Diet Riot

Beetles for breakfast,
Lizards for lunch,
Dragons for dinner —
Crunch
Crunch
Crunch.

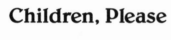

Children, Please

Children, please,
Do not eat worms!
Worms are dirty, full of germs.
Do not chew a caterpillar;
That will only make you iller.
Termites tickle on your tongue,
And they make you overstrung.
Never bite a butterfly;
Tasting one could make you cry.
Don't you know that eating bees
Could inflict a rare disease?
Children, leave your bowls and plates
Free from these invertebrates!

Little-Naughty-Nasty Ned

Little-naughty-nasty Ned
Glued his brother to the bed,
Pinned his father to the floor,
Tied his mother to the door,
Stitched his sister to the curtain —
Bound her hands up to be certain.
In Ned's tiny bedroom closet
Did his uncle he deposit.
Hidden in the rubber plant
Is Ned's favorite maiden aunt.
Now with sadness does Ned moan —
Crying 'cause he's all alone.

Two Gardeners

Tara planted tulip bulbs
And black-eyed Susan seed.
Peter planted light bulbs
So all the worms could read.

Mrs. Mason's Long Red Hair

Mrs. Mason's long red hair
Is shaped just like a sitting chair,
And when she has her friends for tea,
She lets them sit up there for free.
She sprays it seven times a day
With sealing wax from Mandalay,
Then combs it with a wire brush
Until the pile is very plush.
Her darling children love to sneak
Inside her hair for hide-and-seek.
Her husband is a no-good loafer,
Who hopes one day she'll grow a sofa.

Tea Time

Don't slurp or burp
When you drink tea.
Do point your pinky out.
It's very dumb
To use your thumb
To stir the tea about.
Keep elbows off the table, please,
And feet flat on the floor.
And if, good sir,
You wish to stir,
That's what your pinky's for!

Swell Seashell

There was a man who came to dwell
Inside a periwinkle shell.
The space was sparse;
The rent was cheap.
The sound of the sea lulled him to sleep.

Spring Springs

Spring springs.
Summersaults.
Fall falls.
Winter halts.

Doublethink

I think I thought some thoughtful thoughts.
I think I thought up three.
But now I think about those thoughts:
Do those thoughts think of me?

Delicious Wishes

I wish I was taller.
I wish I was strong.
I wish that my short hair
Was silky and long.
I wish I could whistle.
I wish I could sing.
I wish that the winter
Would turn into spring.
I wish I was well read.
I wish I was wise.
I wish that my good looks
Would win me a prize.
I wish I was granted
A wagon of wishes.
I wish that I wasn't
Stuck doing the dishes.

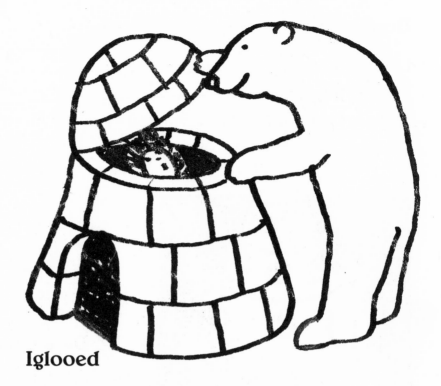

Iglooed

Are igloos glued to the arctic snow
To hold them down when cold winds blow
And keep them from coming all igloose
From nosy polar bears and moose?

The Bipolar Bear

The bipolar bear
Has two heads of hair
And four furry feet —
How it loves to eat
All creatures it sees.
When you see one, *please,*
Be forewarned and beware
Of the bipolar bear.

Be Careful When You Yawn

Be careful when you yawn
That flies don't fly inside,
That caterpillars do not creep
Into your mouth to hide and sleep.
Be wary when your jaw is hung
Of pandas landing on your tongue,
Or seven-masted sailing boats
That choose to cruise across your throat.
Be careful when you yawn!

Smelly Socks

I had a pair of smelly socks.
I filled them with some heavy rocks,
Then tossed them in the deep blue sea,
And there they have my sympathy.

A Silly Young Soldier Named Gannon

A silly young soldier named Gannon
Stuck his big head inside of a cannon.
    When he let out a cough,
    Then the cannon went off.
No more cannons will Gannon be mannin'.

There Was a Young Woman from Boise

There was a young woman from Boise
Whose sneakers were squeaky and noisy.
    She set them to boil
    In sunflower oil,
Then she jogged all the way to New Joisy.

;row on Me

row on me,
You grow on me,
Like fungus growing
On a tree.
You grow on me
Like giant welts.
Why don't you grow
On someone else?

Don't Wanna Be a Grown-Up

Don't wanna be a grown-up,
A fat and overblown-up.
'Cause grown-ups always eat their peas,
Hide their mouths each time they sneeze.
Wear big woolen suits that itch,
Work all day so they'll be rich.
Mind their manners, act polite,
Always smile, never fight.
Talk about the things they've done,
And never ever have much fun.

Chess Mess

They sat down sixty years ago
To play a game of chess.
    But neither one
    Has lost or won —
And never will, I guess.

The Monster in My Mirror

There's a monster in my mirror,
With two beady yellow eyes.
Since I first awoke this morning,
It's been there to my surprise.

It's as wrinkled as a rhino.
It's as hairy as a hound.
And from deep within its belly
Comes a groaning, moaning sound.

Its long teeth are sharp and pointed,
Its fat tongue is shaded blue,
And its mouth is drooling liquid
That resembles airplane glue.

There's a monster in my mirror,
With green horns upon its head.
Tell that monster in my mirror
That I'm going back to bed!

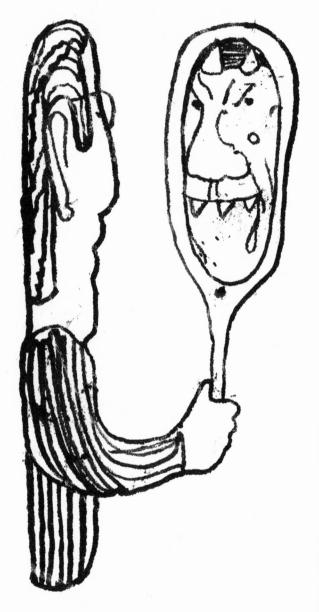

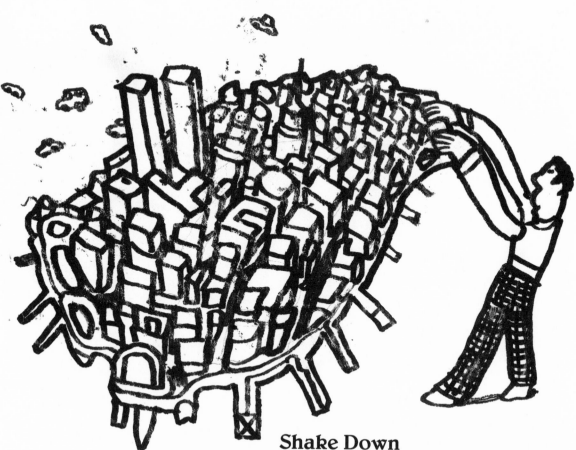

Shake Down

I'd like to shake the city loose
Like some gigantic rug,
To jolt and jar the trucks and cars
and all assorted slugs.

My Building

Eight hundred eighty windows,
And each one looks the same.
Four hundred forty faces,
And not *one* knows my name.

You Don't Say

The early bird gets the worm,
The squeaky wheel gets oiled,
And ugly ogres all agree
That kids taste better boiled.

Barn Swallow

Who told the tale?
Who spun the yarn
About the barn swallow
That swallowed a barn?

Hippopotabus

The giant city bus
Looks like a hippopotamus
That lumbers down the busy street,
With rounded nose and rubber feet.

It swallows people whole
While charging them a toll,
Then carries them about
Until it stops and spits them out.

An Anaconda

An anaconda
Did wanda
And wanda
So far that it forgot
The way back home.
So it roamed
And roamed
Itself into a knot.

Squares

Speaking of squares,
There's no ignoring:
Squares are simple;
Squares are boring.

Turnips Turn Up

Turnips turnup their noses at moles.
Turnips turnup in salad bowls.

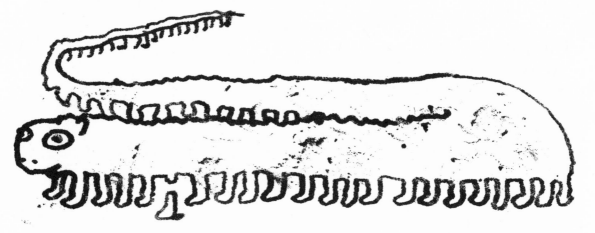

Centipedestrian

See the little centipede walking in a line.
It broke a little leg today but still has ninety-nine.

Silly Nelly

Silly Nelly took a nap
On a sleeping leopard's lap.
From its nap the leopard leaped,
Swallowed Nelly still asleep.
Now inside the leopard's belly
Stays the sleeping, silly Nelly.
Children learn from her mistake:
When near leopards — stay awake!

Ivy

The ivy is growing all over the wall,
Into the window and down to the hall,
Under the desk and over the bed.
The ivy is growing inside of my head.

Meg

Meg in search of an elixir
Jumped inside a concrete mixer.
Nose and toes and arms and legs
All emerged as scrambled Meggs.

Fourteen Men Fainted

Fourteen men fainted
When she walked in the room,
All on account of
Her cheap perfume.

It's Hot! It's Hot!

It's hot!
It's hot!
Not just tepid or warm.
It's hot and a storm
Of mosquitoes is here,
And they're biting my ear
And my arms
And my back
In a vicious attack.
And my skin's soaking wet
With six gallons of sweat,
As mosquitoes I swat
To a bloody flat blot.
And it's hot!
It's hot!

My Mind

My mind is a puzzle.
My mind is a maze.
My mind is closed on Saturdays.

Wednesday's Not with Us Anymore

Wednesday's not with us anymore.
It found the middle of the week a bore.
So after ninety billion years,
Wednesday decided to disappear—
To find a job, to get ahead,
To go to school, to date, to wed.

Why couldn't Monday have left us instead?

Gear Fear

Do you have the strangest fear
Your life is just a little gear
Inside a vast, immense machine
That takes you where you've never been?

Fish Wish

I sat down to a meal of fish,
But it awakened on the dish
And said, "Kid, have you no remorse
To serve fish without tartar sauce?
A slice of lemon is a must —
And bread crumbs lend a tasty crust.
Some saffron rice would taste so nice,
With currants added in for spice.
How I detest a meal so plain.
I shan't be coming back again!"

Pity Little Mortimer

Pity little Mortimer,
They put him in the stocks
For spelling Mississippi wrong
While playing with his blocks.

Mr. Backward

Mr. Backward lives in town.
He never wakes up, he always wakes down.
He eats dessert before his meal.
His plastic plants and flowers are real.
He takes a bath inside his sink
And cleans his clothes with purple ink.
He wears his earmuffs on his nose
And a woolen scarf around his toes.
He loves his gloves worn inside out.
He combs his hair with sauerkraut.
His black dog, Spot, is colored green.
His grandmama is seventeen.
He rakes the leaves still on the trees
And bakes a cake with antifreeze.
He goes to sleep beneath his bed
While wearing slippers on his head.

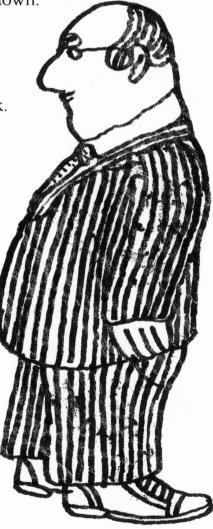

Sleeping Giant

The giant crept
In bed and slept
From midnight till past noon.
His massive head
But broke the bed;
His feet but moved the moon.

Little Mermaid

I know a little mermaid,
Her father is a man.
Her mother is a sardine stuffed
Inside a sardine can.

Knight Fright

Lord have mercy
On Sir Gawaine:
His suit rusted
In the rain.

Smile

It takes a lot of work to frown.
It's easier to smile —
Just take the corners of your mouth
And stretch them for a mile.

Seashells

Seashells
scattered
on
the
whistle   shore,
they   songs,   swept
long   retired   there
day   on   by
all   the   the
But   beach.   ocean,
reach.   once
or   held
leap   creatures
cannot   deep
creep,   inside,
cannot   creeping
seashells   in
Empty
slow-motion.

Tree

Out of the earth
Springs a trunk.
Out of the trunk
Springs a branch.
Out of the branch
Springs a stem.
Out of the stem
Springs a leaf.
Inside the leaf
Are rivers
And oceans
Of life.

A Hippo's Hip

A hippo's hip
Could sink a ship.
Its back could crack a street.
But a hippo's rear,
I truly fear,
Could sink the British fleet.

Birthday

I got two dozen toys today,
A sweater, and a vest.
My brother Bart got nothing.
(That's what I love the best.)

Generals

Generals in general
Have medals and stars,
Tassels and ribbons,
Stripes and bars,
Badges and buttons,
And eagles galore.
But what's *that*
Got to do with war?

I Friz, I Froze

It waz so cold
I friz, I froze
My earz, my ize,
My noze, my toze.
My kneez did freeze
Az hard az stone.
My head'z a frozen
Ize cream cone.

Fog Flub

In the misty morning fog
I mistook Mother
For a frog.

Melt Down

Beneath the sun
The snowmen melt.
They sink without a sound.
But snowmen never really die;
They just move underground.

Most Mustaches

Mustaches curl,
Mustaches swirl
Like the shell of a snail
Or the tail of a whale.
Some are bushy and broad;
Others sharp as a sword.
But there's one thing I knows:
Most mustaches goes
Under somebody's nose.

Comb Poem

A man who hadn't any hair
Took out his comb
To comb the air.

Auntlers

My aunt grew auntlers overnight.
They gave my uncle Grant a fright!
But Auntie's glad the auntlers grew —
She posts up notes of things to do.

School Cafeteria

Nothing is drearier than my school cafeteria —
The food there is really the pits.
The bread is as hard as a brick in a yard;
The cake is all crumbled to bits.
The rotten old cheeses can give you diseases;
The pudding is rancid and runny.
And if you should dare to bite into a pear,
The taste is so bad it's not funny.
The chicken and rice are served cold as ice;
The soups could send groups to the nurse.
The carrots and peas make you whimper and wheeze;
The broccoli comes with a curse.
The pizza, I'm told, is covered with mold;
The salad is pallid and stale.
The dried-out roast beef fills your belly with grief;
They're taking the cook off to jail.
The citrus fruit cup will make you throw up;
The cookies are made out of clay.
The mere thought of lunch
Makes my weak stomach scrunch —
But it's still the best part of the day.

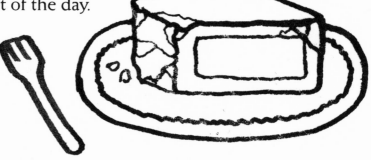

They Put Me in the Stupid Class

They put me in the stupid class
When history I did not pass.
But I'll show them,
Just wait and see —
I'll graduate with a degree
In economic management.
And then I'll run for president,
Where in a landslide I will win.
Then heads will roll and tails will spin.
I'll round up all my teachers fast
And put *them* in the stupid class.

Ben Bent

Ben bent over backward to please,
Until his head went through his knees.
Pleasing him and her and you —
But now bent Ben is stuck like glue.

Noodles

Noodles and peas,
Noodles and cheese,
And for all you cannibals:
Noodles and knees.

Tall or Small

Some are tall
And some are small,
But one thing I have found:
From any height,
Severe or slight,
Their feet just reach the ground.

Heavy Head

If you have a heavy head,
Rest it on the floor instead.
You will see things all anew,
And you'll get a worm's-eye view.

What an Elephant's Trunk Is Good For

Spraying showers,
Picking flowers.
Moving your bed,
Smacking your head.
Getting cats out of trees,
Picking you up by the knees.
Holding files,
Throwing a Frisbee seventeen miles.
Giving a hug,
Squashing a bug.
Raking leaves,
Catching thieves.
Painting a wall,
Playing basketball.
(It's easy to dunk when your nose is a trunk.)

Whale Tale

We are trapped inside the mouth of a whale,
But we don't mind it one bit:
There's plenty of heat,
And fish to eat,
And lots of room to sit.

The Ho

The humble Ho
Is lying low
In the bottom of a cup.
But you will find
It doesn't mind,
For things are looking up.

Belly Roll

Frank drank root beer
By the bowl —
Now watch his barrel
Belly roll.

Mr. Rose's Balancing Shows

In Mr. Rose's balancing shows
He balances balls above his nose,
Above the balls two turtle doves,
Above the doves a baseball glove,
Above the glove his lady love —
Ain't that the greatest
You've ever heard of?

Shoe View

There was an old lady who lived in a shoe.

       Pew!

       Pew!

       Pew!

       Pew!

       Pew!

       Pew!

       Pew!

News Coverage

For when it rains
And when it pours —
That's what a good
Newspaper's for.

Gloves and Galoshes

I'm wearing my gloves and galoshes
Outside where the wet weather washes
   The trees and the street,
   All the grass 'neath my feet,
And a spot where a person was nauseous.

Self Change

Mr. Myer began to tire
Of how his body looked.
So he began to wiggle
Till his body parts all shook.
He knocked his nose down to his toes,
His ears down to his thighs,
His calves and shins up to his chin,
His elbows to his eyes.
All parts and places were moved to spaces
You do not often see 'em.
And now his bits and pieces sit
Inside of a museum.

The Incredible Shrinking Poem

I washed

this poem in
the bathroom
sink, and now
it shrinks &
shrinks &
shrinks.

Jupiter

Jeff says the largest planet is Jupiter.
Simon says Saturn, but Simon is stupider.

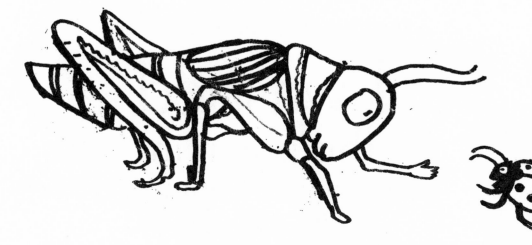

Life in the Grass Lane

Do bugs and beetles in the grass
Give signs and signals as they pass?
Do grasshoppers and centipedes
Slow down as ladybugs proceed?
Or do they find it too much bother
And simply crawl upon each other?

Flea Fur All

Fur fills fleas with glee:
In fur they feel so fancy-free.
They prance and dance in ecstasy.
In cheetahs, chipmunks, and chimpanzees:
Fur fills fleas with glee.

The Thin Man

I know
a man
who is
so thin,
you never
know which
room he's in.
He looks
just like
a walking stick.
Near him
a fishing pole
looks thick.
The slightest
breeze will
blow him down.
He has
no shadow
on the ground.
Come meet
him now
while he's still here.
No, wait —
I think
he's disappeared!

The Fat Man

I know a man who's so obese,
His feet weigh fifty pounds apiece.
Two hundred times a day he snacks;
Beneath his feet the sidewalk cracks.
Each time this man swims in the ocean,
A tidal wave is set in motion.
He has to squeeze inside a door;
His mattress sinks down to the floor.
The kids all call him Roly Poly;
His middle name is Ravioli.
He wears a tent instead of pants;
His waistline is a huge expanse.
Come meet him now!
Come shake his hand!
But help us first get him to stand.

A Deer Mouse

A deer mouse on a turtle's shell
Went searching for a wishing well
So it could wish for all its needs:
A million pounds of nuts and seeds.

Inch by Inch

While I was climbing
Up a tree,
A green
Inchworm
Was climbing up me.

A Fire-Breathing Dragon

A fire-breathing dragon
Would make a precious pet —
It's great for grilling hot dogs
And drying clothes all wet.

It gladly guards the house and yard
From burglars in the street.
On winter nights how it delights
To warm your frozen feet.

It eats unwanted guests for lunch
And munches noisy neighbors.
Insistent salesmen at the door,
A hungry dragon savors.

A dragon is a noble beast,
A perfect primal pet.
The only trick
Is when it's sick,
Don't let it eat the vet.

Hiram Zabriskie

Hiram Zabriskie was fretful and frisky.
He couldn't sit still in his seat.
He'd turn somersaults drinking strawberry malts
While juggling jugs with his feet.
His big nose would jiggle;
His eyeballs would wiggle;
His huge ears would wriggle and wave.
And I've heard it said
That when he was dead,
Poor Hiram jumped out of his grave.

Trouble Bubble Bath

There's trouble in my bubble bath —
It's time to disembark.
Beneath the soap and suds there swims
The cleanest, meanest shark.

Tuba

Tom plays tuba
In his tub,
With his scuba . . .
Blub
Blub
Blub.

Commas

Do commas have mommas
Who teach them to pause,
Who comfort and calm them,
And clean their sharp claws?
Who tell them short stories
Of uncommon commas
And send them to bed
In their comma pajamas?

Norse

Norse is as big as a horse.
He wears iron horseshoes, of course.
    He bangs them in slowly,
    Screaming words most unholy,
Then races out on the racecourse.

Fred and Sue

My best friend, Fred,
Has rocks in his head—
He must have more than thirty.
And good old Fred,
He washes his head
Whenever the rocks get dirty.
My sister, Sue,
Went up to Fred
And said, "I beg your pardon,
But will you take these violets
To make a nice rock garden?"

Doughnutty

Kate ate doughnuts by the box
Till her teeth turned into rocks,
Till her brains turned into bread,
Till a hole grew in her head.

Book Schnook

Sidney Schellman is a schnook —
Went to sleep inside a book.
Sidney sprang this silly scheme
So he could read inside his dream.

Twinkle, Twinkle

Twinkle, twinkle, little star,
How I wonder what you are —
    A sphere of incandescent gas
    Spinning round a nuclear mass.
Twinkle, twinkle, little star,
How I wonder what you are.

Our Bicycle Built for Two

There's nothing we would rather do
Than ride our bicycle built for two.
But something's wrong, something's askew:
We don't know what.
Do you?

The Fastest Car

The fastest car I ever saw
Was just a blur on Highway Four.

I Taught My Cat

I taught my cat to play piano,
To ride a bike,
To sing soprano.
To drive, to draw,
To paint, to plow —
And she taught me how
To meow.

Corny

If you were born
With ears of corn,
You couldn't hear
Your mother dear.
How could you listen
To your sweet mother
With corn in one ear
And out the other?

Tired Hair

If you're tired of your hair,
Rope it to a rocking chair.

Hang it from a chandelier;
Wrap it round a fishing pier.

Tie it into fifty knots;
Dye it green with purple spots.

Hitch it to a railroad train;
Stitch it with your middle name.

Mail it first class in a letter;
Weave it in your cashmere sweater.

Comb it with a garden rake;
Mix it in a chocolate cake.

Feed it to a hungry pig;
Then go out and buy a wig.

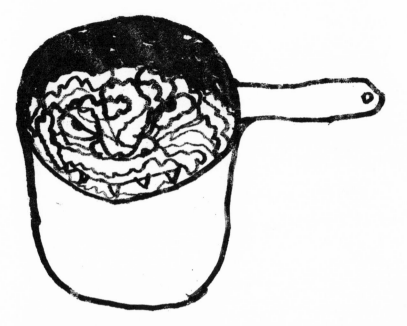

Pease-Porridge Not

Pease-porridge hot,
Pease-porridge cold,
Pease-porridge in the pot,
Nine days old.

Would YOU eat porridge
Nine days old,
Hard as rock,
And covered with mold?
Growing fur
And turning blue?
Perhaps pease-porridge
Would rather eat YOU!

What the Garbage Truck Ate for Breakfast Today

Two turkey bones
A cracked-up clock,
Four orange peels
A soiled sock.
Tuesday's news
Aluminum foil,
Seven quarts
Of motor oil.
Thirty prune pits
Dirty diapers,
A pair of broken
Windshield wipers.
An old kazoo
A moldy poster,
A 1967 toaster.
A tattered girdle
A turtleneck . . .
And never had to pay the check.

Bacteria

Bacteria infect:
Bacteria inflame.
Some are so rotten, they don't have a name.

The Bully

There's a bully in our class —
He pushed Polly in the grass.
He kicked Kevin in the shin
And poked Peter with a pin.
On the arm he pinched Louise.
How Lucille he loved to tease.
He stole all of Johnny's money
And thought tripping Todd was funny.
Poor Marie, he pulled her hair.
Harold's homework he did tear.
He gave Alistair a punch
And ate Marguerita's lunch.
Then one day he hit Clarisse —
May his poor soul rest in peace.

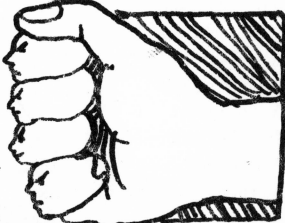

Ghostmobile

Sit down inside my ghostmobile,
Extraordinary mostmobile.
It needs no oil, grease, or gas.
It has no rubber, steel, or glass.
To start it up here's all you do:
Turn out the lights and then shout "BOO!"

How Do Ghosts Get Their Sheets Clean?

How do ghosts get their sheets clean?
Do most ghosts own a washing machine?
Or do they clean them in a tub —
First pour in soap, then scrub, scrub, scrub?
Hang them to dry right on their head?
Without clean sheets they'd rather be dead!

Cars Are Creatures

Cars are creatures
Of the road:
Steel-skinned,
Glass-eyed,
Tire-toed.
Guzzling gas,
Growling
As they pass.
Taillights blink-
　　　blink-
　　　　blinking.
Tailpipes stinking.
(What are they thinking?)
Through day and dark
They ride,
Coughing carbon
Monoxide.
And when they lose their spark,
They slowly park
And soundly
Sleep outside.

What

What has fourteen hairy legs?
What lays purple pointed eggs?
What has spines along its back?
What eats children for a snack?
What is more than ten feet tall?
What has eyes like basketballs?
What has seven swirling tails?
What has poison on its nails?
What has stringy, long green hairs?

I don't know, but it's coming upstairs!

Rain Check

Rain, rain,
Go away.
Come again
Another day —
Like Friday
The sixteenth of May
(My sister Sarah's
Sixth birthday).

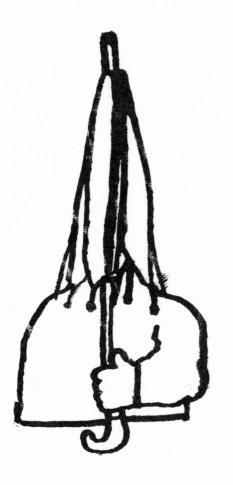

Weather It

Monday it rained,
Tuesday it snowed,
Wednesday it drizzled,
Thursday wind blowed.
Friday brought fog,
Saturday hail.
Sunday the weatherman
Was thrown into jail.

Father Sky and Mother Earth

Said Father Sky to Mother Earth,
"How wonderfully wide
You are in girth.
I love your verdant rolling hills —
Your lofty mountains
Give me thrills.
At times I wonder how it feels
To have a stream
Run round one's heels.
And is it odd that maple trees
Can sprout up out
Of both your knees?"

Said Mother Earth to Father Sky,
"How bright you are,
And light and high.
You have the right to feel so proud
Of all your
Cirro-stratus clouds.
You shine in ever-changing hues,
From tangerines
To cobalt blues.
You give me such delightful weather —
How nice that we
Could get together."

Foothills

We climbed the foothills of North Dakota —
Zeeks!
Zounds!
What an odor!

Styropoem

I think I've never
Seen a poem
To praise a piece
of Styrofoam.
I've waited years —
I'm waiting still.
I guess I never
Ever
Will.

Turn on the Sunshine

Turn on the sunshine.
Turn on the sand.
Let's go to the beach
And all get tanned.

Lost Head

I'm sorry I got angry.
I guess I lost my head.
It really doesn't matter —
I'll borrow yours instead.
I'll have it back by Friday.
You won't miss it at all.
Until then you can borrow
My brother's basketball.

The Serpent That Lives in Loch Ness

The serpent that lives in Loch Ness
Is sixty yards long, more or less.
    It swallowed my mother,
    My father, and brother,
To teach them togetherness.

Witch Whisk

A wicked witch upon her broom
Swept in the window of my room.
I socked her nose; I knocked her knee —
But she stuck out her tongue at me.
I smacked her back; I shook her shin —
She smiled at me a toothless grin.
I pricked her arm; I kicked her calf —
She cackled me a horrid laugh.
I asked that witch to clean my room —
She flew away upon her broom.

Mr. and Mrs. Glatt

Mr. Glatt is very fat,
And Mrs. Glatt is thin —
So when they stand together
They make a perfect 10.

Mr. Britton

Mr. Britton bought a bowler;
Got run over by a steamroller.
That roller rolled his features flat;
Now he needs another hat.

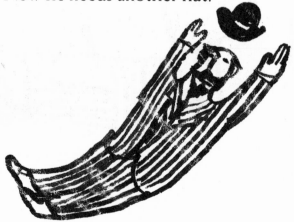

Mrs. Mary Musty

Mrs. Mary Musty,
Finicky and fussy,
Covered her dog
So it wouldn't get dusty.
Covered her nails
So they wouldn't get rusty.
Covered her sweater
So it wouldn't sweat.
Covered the sea
So it wouldn't get wet.
Covered the sun
So it wouldn't set.

One Potato Chip

You can't eat *one* potato chip,
For soon as one chip hits your lip,
You pine to dine a second piece —
Then third and fourth and fifth at least.
And soon you chew chips by the dozen.
You steal them from your second cousin.
You gulp them down right in the pack
And later buy a ten-pound sack.
You chomp on chips then by the truck.
(Your appetite has run amok.)
And later take the liberty
To swallow the whole factory.
Until at last your feast is done —
You couldn't, wouldn't eat just *one*.
You ate far more than you should oughta,
Then swallowed fifty quarts of water.

Suburbia

Welcome to suburbia,
Where life is so superbia.
A swimming pool in every yard —
The living's easy, never hard.
The houses here all look the same,
Like plastic pieces in a game.
Our schools are smart;
Our streets are clean.
Our perfect lawns
Are always green.
The people here are trouble-free
But die from the monotony.

There Used to Be

There used to be a forest here,
With turtle eyes and rabbit ears.
These woods were full
Of great green places,
But now they're gone
For parking spaces,
Concrete islands,
Shopping malls,
Self-serve gas
And bathroom stalls,
Crowds of people,
Clouds of smoke,
Ceramic frogs
That never croak.

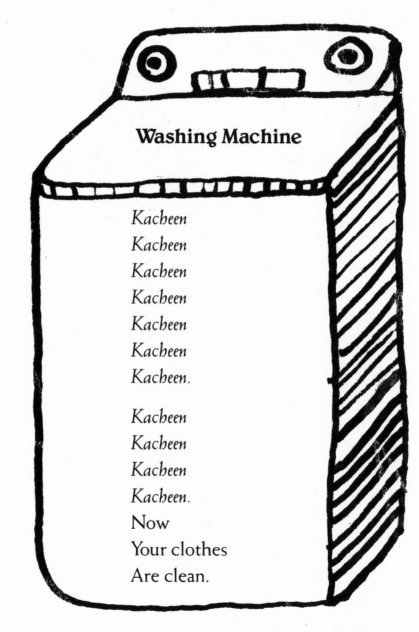

Washing Machine

Kacheen
Kacheen
Kacheen
Kacheen
Kacheen
Kacheen
Kacheen.

Kacheen
Kacheen
Kacheen
Kacheen.
Now
Your clothes
Are clean.

Something's There

Something's there
In the Frigidaire—
Something long forgotten,
Something ruined and rotten.
Way in the back—
Green and black.
Behind the eggs—
I think it has legs.
Something stale—
Do I see a tail?
Check it out—
Is that a snout?

Let's go eat out.

Do unto Every Vegetable

Do unto every vegetable
As it does unto you.
Be extra nice before you slice
Each up into a stew.
Show courtesy to broccoli,
Be kind to rind of melon;
Speak gingerly to celery,
Resist all forms of yellin'.
Take care that carrots are amused,
Be sweet to sweet potatoes;
And learn to cope with cantaloupe,
Talk tender to tomatoes.
On cauliflower shower praise,
Of leeks do speak with grace;
Don't dare be harsh with sprouts or squash,
Stay mellow with all maize.

Do unto every vegetable
As it does unto you.
Remember each with warm regards
With every bite you chew.

There Was an Old Woman Named Rose

There was an old woman named Rose,
Who carried a crab on her nose.
    One day she screamed, "Gosh!
    While I'm doing the wash,
I can use it to hold up my clothes!"

There Was a Young Woman from Nome

There was a young woman from Nome,
Who wore an eleven-pound comb.
    Each time she did curtsy,
    How her backbone did hurtsy,
So she's keeping her huge comb at home.

Elephant Pants

I feel that all the elephants
Should have to wear a pair of pants.
It's most offensive to my eye
To see these naked beasts go by.
That wolverines walk in the nude
Strikes me as being very rude.
And I would wish a polar bear
Equip itself with underwear.
For goodness' sake, I think it's best
That hooded cobras wear a vest.
And don't you think a boar looks better
Inside a pink acrylic sweater?
I'd love to see a nanny goat
Put on a warm Afghani coat.
And couldn't bulls of every breed
Slip into woolly suits of tweed?
Why not insist that spiders sport
A pair of smart Bermuda shorts?
I think we all have had enough
Of barracudas in the buff.
For beasts of every shape and size,
The time is now — so customize!

Motorgoat

A goat with a motor
Could go to Dakota,
Could motor up mountains with ease.
But if that goat's motor
Don't work like it oughta,
He'll feast on that motor with cheese.

My Monster

I saw a monster
Ghastly and green.
I saw a monster
Nasty and mean.
I saw a monster,
A horrible creature.
That's no monster —
That's my teacher!

The Lazy Man

There was a man who stayed in bed
Till mushrooms sprouted from his head.
He soundly slept for years and years,
While flowers blossomed from his ears.
His arms grew covered with green moss,
As tiny termites slowly crossed
Between his legs and round his toes,
While bugs and ants crawled in his nose.
A robin stole hair from his chest
To warm its little feathered nest.
And slowly on his skinny knee,
There grew an elderberry tree.
A thousand years he simply lied
Until his body petrified.
All of his skin and flesh and bones
Had turned to pebbles, rocks, and stones,
This lazy man without a care,
Who someday wasn't even there.

Madame Doubletalk

I said, "Madame, have you the time?"
   "I don't," said she. "It's ten past nine."
"And do you think that it might rain?"
   "No, no, I see a hurricane."
"Where can I catch a downtown bus?"
   "Right here, a hundred miles from us."
"Do you speak French, by any chance?"
   "Not me," she said. *"Commence la danse."*
"What do you like to do for fun?"
   "To stay indoors, out in the sun."
"How is your health? How do you feel?"
   "Not well at all — as strong as steel."
"Do you do calisthenics much?"
   "I jump and run and use a crutch."
"What is your secret of success?"
   "Wear simple clothes and overdress."
"Good-bye, madame, I have to go."
   "Good-bye, good-bye. Hello, hello."

What the Wind Swept Away Today

A snow white feather from a dove,
A finger from a long lost glove.
Someone's homework (graded D),
A purple leaf (off a tree).
A parking ticket torn in half,
A battered, tattered photograph.
A lucky fortune-cookie note,
A pencil drawing of a boat.
A corner of a map of Greece,
A postcard written in Chinese.
Page three hundred twenty-two
From a book on Timbuktu.
A ribbon swept up from my hair,
And my little sister Claire.

Destinations

All that wiggles, jiggles, and jostles
In the end will just be fossils.

Index of Titles

Index of First Lines

Grateful acknowledgments to:

Nancy Phethean for her serendipitous suggestion of the title.
Robin Cruise for her careful and creative copyediting.
Anna Roach for her enthusiastic encouragement.
Kaelin Chappell for her dedicated design.
Michael Farmer for his valuable vision.
Marvin Bileck for his illuminating instruction.
Barbara Fenton for her unwavering wisdom.
Juliana McIntyre for her perceptive perusal.
David Hough for his daily diligence.
Warren Wallerstein for his perfectionist production.
And Allyn Johnston for her courageous confidence.